D0924728

The Holy Land from Above

Aerial photography by Ron Gafni

"The Holy Land From Above" takes us on a journey to some of Israel's most known locations, holy and secular, east and west, sharing this magnificent refreshing beauty as seen from a unique vantage point.

Sky Pics .co.il

ישראל במבט מהאוויר

צילומים: רון גפני

The Holy Land from Above
Aerial Photography by Ron Gafni

Photography: Ron Gafni
Editing & Production: SkyPics.co.il
Design: Amir Rom

Thanks to:
Michael Golan, Reuven G.,
my airborne colleagues.
ArtinClay studio,
Hot air balloons: Rize.co.il

+972-(0)9-8650068
info@SkyPics.co.il
www.SkyPics.co.il
ישראל בספרי מתנה

©All Rights Reserved No part of this publication
may be reproduced, photographed, recorded,
translated, stored in a retrieval system, broadcast
or recorded in any way or by any electronic
means, optical, mechanical or otherwise,
whatsoever. Use for reviews of any type of the
material contained in this book is
absolutely forbidden without the specific and
prior permission of the holders of the right.

ISBN 9789659118014
Made in Israel

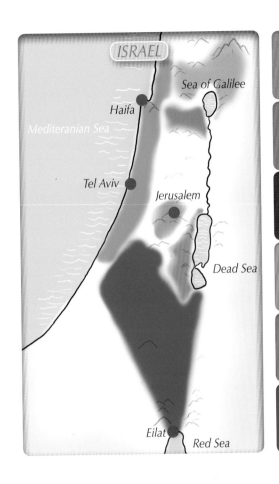

ISRAEL

Sea of Galilee

Haifa

Mediteranian Sea

Tel Aviv

Jerusalem

Dead Sea

Eilat

Red Sea

Jerusalem

∧ *Old City walls: Jaffa Gate and Tower of David, near by in the center,*
The Holy Sepulcher Domes at the end of Via Dolorosa

Jerusalem City and behind the Judean Desert, the Dead Sea with the Edom mountains in the horizon. >

⋀ *The Western Wall, the last remnant of the Temple, the most significant site in the world for the Jewish people* ⟩

< Jerusalem >

*Yad Vashem,
The Holocaust
Martyr's and Heroe's
Remembrance
Authority >*

*Monument to the
Jewish Soldiers
and Partisans >*

∧ Hall of Remembrance

*The Shrine of the
Book and model
of the 2nd Temple,
Israel Museum
>*

< **Jerusalem** >

Church of All Nations at the Kidron Valley

∧ Inside The Church of the Holy Sepulcher,
the Christian quarter at the Old City
of Jerusalem

∧ The Nativity Church, where Jesus was
born at Bethlehem

∧ The Old and New City skyline

Church of Mary Magdalene near by the Garden of Gethsemane >

⋀ *The market at the Old City*

Jerusalem at night, Dome of The Rock on the Moriha Mt. >

Dormition Church
on Mount Zion
>

/\ The Russian monastery (Moskovia), Ein Kerem

/\ Mishkenot Sha'ananim & Montefiore
Windmill, first Jewish settlement
outside the Old City

Saint John the Baptist Church, Ein Kerem >

Galilee & Golan

∧ Tabgha, the Fish and loaves miracle site just below the Mt. of Beatitudes

Arbel Cliff above the ancient city of Migdal (Magdala),
The Sea of Galilee and behind the Golan Heights >

< Galilee & Golan >

Nazareth,
The Church of
Annunciation
in the center of
the city
>

/\ *Kfar Kana, "The Wedding Church"*

Mt. of Beatitudes, the place where Jesus delivered the Sermon >

< Galilee & Golan >

∧ Capernaum, center of Jesus public ministry in the Galilee

Yardenit, the baptismal site at the Jordan River
∨

This Fish and Loaves Byzantine mosaic, preserved under the Tabgha Church. >

Tiberias and Sea of Galilee >

∧ Amud Canyon, natural structure inside the canyon

∧ The Zavitan Falls

The Meshushim (hexagonal columns) Pool at the Yehudia Stream >

< **Galilee & Golan** >

< *Mt. Hermon, above Golan Heights* ∧

The Hula natural resort, National Park since 1998: commemorating the swamp that was dried out by Jewish pioneers during the early 20th century
∨

Hot air balloon above the Jezreel Valley overlooking Nazareth and The Lower Galilee mountains >

Dead Sea & Judea Desert

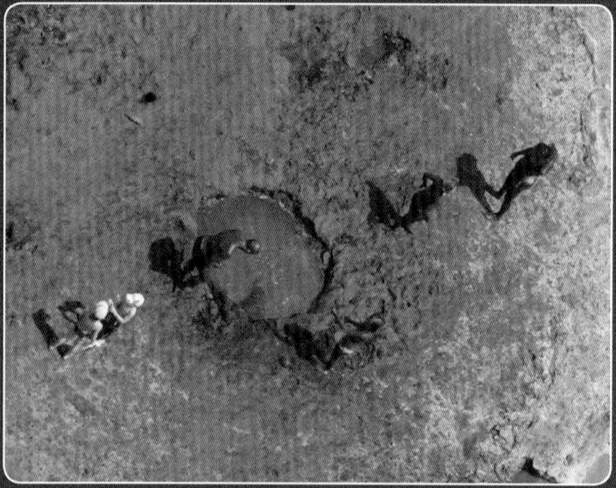

Mineral mud, found along the banks of the Dead Sea

Dead Sea hotels, Spa, health and recreational tourist centers >

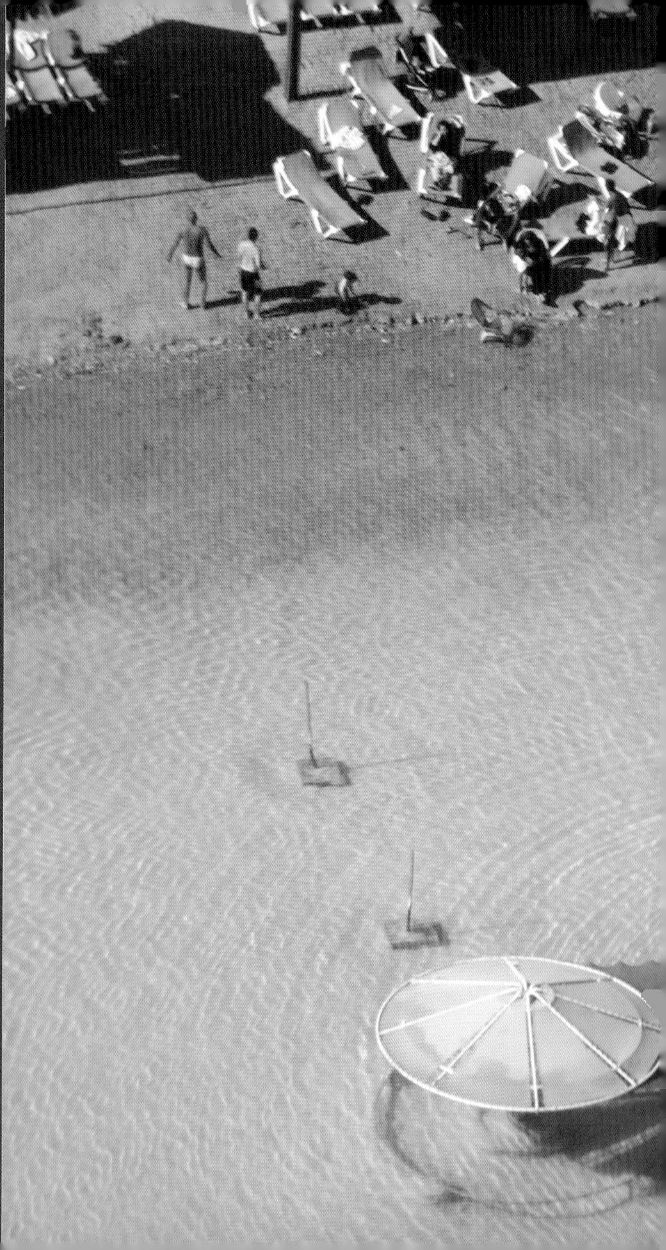

< Dead Sea & Judea Desert >

∧ Masada, first built by Herod
the Great, rises more than 400
meters above the Dead Sea

∧ Herodium Fortress, built by Herod
as one in a chain of fortresses along
the Judean Desert

∧ Qumran: the ancient settlement
near the cave where the Dead
Sea Scrolls were hidden

Masada's story of courage and unity which
became a legend for the people of Israel

>

< Dead Sea & Judea Desert >

Dead Sea hotels below the Judean Desert ridge, in the canyon behind there's a fresh water pond originating at Ein Bokek >

Dead Sea shore >

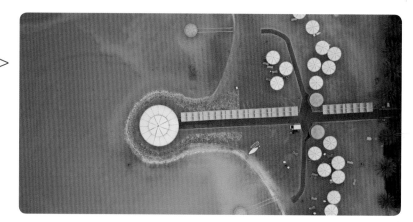

Retreating shores leaving behind colourful sink holes >

< Dead Sea & Judea Desert >

∧ Water canal at the Dead Sea

∧ Sunken boat covered with salt

Saint George Monastery, Wadi Qelt >

< Dead Sea & Judea Desert >

Λ Mar Saba Monastery

Sedom Mountain above the Dead Sea >

Coast Line

△ Fly by Tel Aviv coast line

Acre. The walls, fortresses, citadels, churches and
mosques of the city tells the history of the many
rulers who governed and fought for it >

∧ Haifa bay

∧
Haifa, The Bahai World Center Gardens dominate the
area of Mount Carmel directly above the sea port

⋀ Caesarea, Roman Amphitheatre

Caesarea, Old palace and Hippodrome >

The Old City of Jaffa
∨

Jaffa port and Tel Aviv coast line >

Sunset over a popular Tel Aviv beach >

∧ Port of Haifa, functional for the past 2,300 years

∧ Next to Netanya beach

Northern valleys

∧ *Flower fields on the Issaschar Heights*

Mount Tabor, Site of the battle between Barak and the army of Jabin, commanded by Sisera. The Church of Transfiguration rests on the top of the mountain >

Gilboa mountains
above the
Beit Shean Valley
<

Beit Shean ruins, one of the most ancient
cities called Scythopolis, the capital of the
Decapolis (10 Roman cities in this region),
destroyed in the earthquake of 363 AC.
∨

Asi River, running through Kibbutz Nir David >

Megiddo
("Armageddon")
ruins of ancient cities
below Mt. Carmel
>

Nahalal village at the Jezreel valley >

Migrating birds at Beit Shean Valley, world phenomenon where each year millions of migrating birds cross Israel >

Almond blossom during "Tu b'Shvat" holiday time >

⋀ *Fish ponds at the Beit Shean valley*

*Sachne, a natural pond located
below the Gilboa mountains* >

Eilat & Southern Deserts

∧ Eilat, Dolphin Reef

Eilat, Northern Beach >

∧ Special army unit symbols at Katum Mt.
  in the Ramon Crater

∧ Ramon Crater's magnificently colored soil

Wheat fields in the dry streams of the Negev Desert >

Peanut threshing in the
Northern Negev fields
>

Hot Air Balloon over the Negev open fields >

Λ Motorcycle random trails generating a
"Miro" like picture, Arava near Eilat

V Karate training in the Negev, Kibbutz Kfar Menachem

Southern desert Anemones (kalaniot) in blossom >

The Holy Land from above

Aerial photography by Ron Gafni

About the photographer:

Ron Gafni (1970, Kibbutz Gaash) works as a professional photographer after more than a decade as a software engineer in Israel's High-Tech Industry. Over the years of flying in different aircrafts, he has accumulated and captured most visible treasures of the land and its people. Gafni shoots mainly aerial photos, as well as urban and scenic landscapes. Some of Gafni's extensive work has been published in the book " Israel From Above" and other albums showing Israel at its best. "The Holy Land From Above" with its newest design is his latest book.

photo: Nadav Hayun